THE WORD DETECTIVE

IN GERMAN

With Easy Pronunciation Guide

Heather Amery and Sonja Osthecker
Illustrated by Colin King

Pronunciation Guide by Gillian Adams

Inspektor Nomen und die geheimnisvollen Vorgänge auf dem Markt

Inspector Noun and the market mystery

der Markt

das Gemüse **das Obst**

Nomen geht auf den Markt, um einen Dieb zu finden.
Noun goes to market to find a thief.

die Kirschen*

Er denkt: ,,Wer ißt die Kirschen
He thinks, "Who is eating the cherries

die Erdbeeren*

und die Erdbeeren
and the strawberries

die Himbeeren*

und die Himbeeren?''
and the raspberries?''

die Ananas

Er sieht sich eine Ananas an,
He looks at a pineapple,

die Melone

läßt eine Melone fallen
drops a melon

der Apfel

und ißt einen Apfel.
and eats an apple.

die Orangen*

Er geht an den Orangen,.
He walks past the oranges,

die Zitronen*

den Zitronen
the lemons

die Aprikosen*

und den Aprikosen vorbei.
and the apricots.

die Birnen*

Er schaut die Birnen,
He looks at the pears,

die Trauben*

die Trauben
at the grapes

die Bananen*

und die Bananen an.
and the bananas.

der Pfirsich

die Pampelmuse

die Pflaumen*

Er bleibt stehen, um auf einen Pfirsich zu drücken und um eine Pampelmuse und ein Paar Pflaumen zu
He stops to squeeze a peach,   buy a grapefruit   and some plums. **kaufen.**

4

die Erbsen*

„Wer hat die Erbsen
"Who has been eating the peas

die Bohnen*

und die Bohnen
and the beans

der Salat

und den Salat gegessen?"
and the lettuce?"

die Kartoffeln*

Nomen untersucht die Kartoffeln
Noun looks at the potatoes

die Möhren*

und die Möhrer
and the carrots

die Kohlköpfe*

und die Kohlköpfe.
and the cabbages.

die Tomate

Er tritt auf eine Tomate,
He steps on a tomato,

die Pilze*

stößt ein Körbchen voller Pilze
knocks down some mushrooms

die Wasserkresse

und einen Eimer mit Wasserkresse um.
and kicks over the watercress.

die Rüben*

Er schaut hinter den Rüben
He peers round the turnips

der Rosenkohl

und dem Rosenkohl hervor
and the sprouts

die Rote Bete

und kriecht an der Roten Bete vorbei.
and crawls past the beetroot.

die Sellerie

Er geht an der Sellerie vorbei,
He walks past the celery,

die Radieschen*

und sieht sich die Radieschen
and looks at the radishes

die Zwiebeln*

und die Zwiebeln an.
and the onions.

der Lauch

Er rutscht auf einer Lauch aus,
He slips on a leek,

der Blumenkohl

stolpert über einen Blumenkohl
trips over a cauliflower

die Diebe*

und findet die Diebe.
and finds the thieves.

Inspektor Nomen und die gestohlenen Diamanten
Inspector Noun and the stolen diamonds

das Schiff

Inspektor Nomen fährt zu dem Schiff.
Inspector Noun drives to the ship.

das Fallreep

Er geht das Fallreep hinauf
He walks up the gang plank

der Kapitän

und spricht mit dem Kapitän.
and talks to the captain.

die Diamanten*

der Dieb

die Frau

Der Kapitän erzählt ihm, daß einige Diamanten von einem Dieb gestohlen worden sind. Aber eine Frau
The captain says some diamonds have been stolen by a thief. But a woman saw him.
hat ihn gesehen.

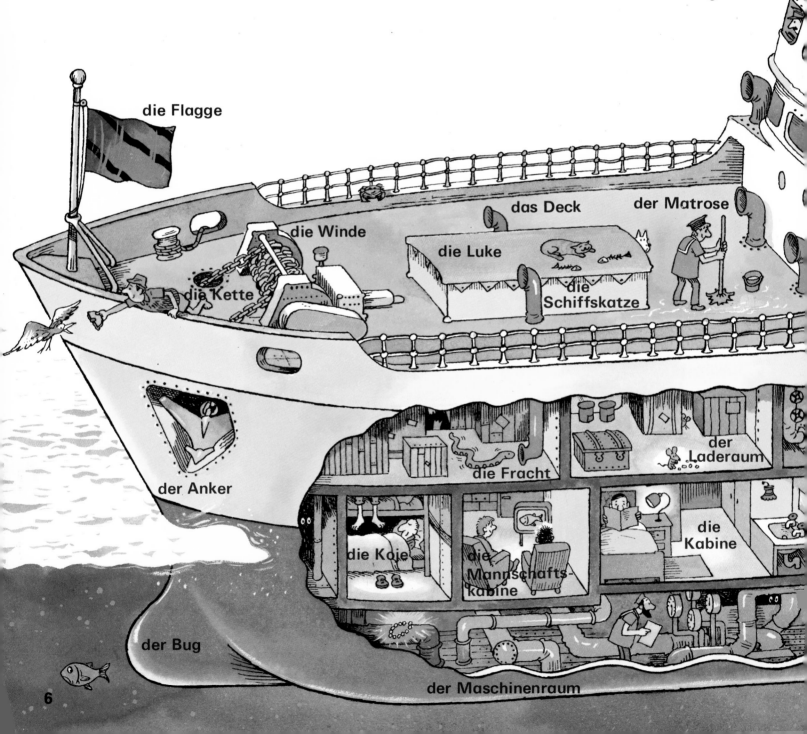

die Flagge

das Deck

der Matrose

die Winde

die Luke

die Schiffskatze

die Kette

der Anker

die Fracht

der Laderaum

die Kabine

die Koje

die Mannschafts-kabine

der Bug

der Maschinenraum

6

das Deck

Nomen schleicht über das Deck
Noun creeps along the deck

der Mann

und fängt den Mann.
and catches the man.

die Taschen*

Aber seine Taschen sind leer.
But his pockets are empty.

der Mast

der Schornstein

die Möve

die Kommando-
brücke

der Aufenthalts-
raum

**Der Dieb hat die Diamanten auf dem Schiff versteckt.
Kannst du sie finden?**
The thief has hidden the diamonds in the ship.
Can you find them?

der Liegestuhl

die Rettungsboote*

die Reling

der Küchenchef

der Kellner

die Küche

der Speisesaal

das Heck

das Badezimmer

die Dusche

die Treppe

die Bullaugen*

das Steuerruder

die Schiffsschraube

die Leiter

der Maschinist

Wachtmeister Verb hat einen schweren Tag
Sergeant Verb has a busy day

schlafen

Verb liegt im Bett und schläft.
Verb sleeps in bed.

aufwachen

Er wacht auf
He wakes up

steigen

und steigt aus dem Bett.
and climbs out of bed.

aufdrehen

Er dreht die Wasserkräne auf,
He turns on the taps,

waschen

wäscht sich die Hände
washes his hands

reiben

und reibt sein Gesicht trocken.
and rubs his face.

putzen

Er putzt sich die Zähne,
He cleans his teeth,

ausziehen

zieht seinen Schlafanzug aus,
takes off his pyjamas,

anziehen

zieht seine Kleidung an
puts on his clothes

bürsten

und bürstet sich das Haar.
and brushes his hair.

rutschen

Verb rutscht das Geländer hinunter
Verb slides down the banisters

essen

und ißt dann sein Frühstück.
and then eats his breakfast.

trinken

Er trinkt seinen Kaffee,
He drinks his coffee,

lesen

liest die Zeitung
reads the newspaper

fallen lassen

und läßt einen Teller fallen.
and drops a plate.

füttern

Er füttert den Kanarienvogel,
He feeds the canary,

schließen

schließt das Fenster
closes the window

öffnen

und öffnet die Tür.
and opens the door.

fahren

Er fährt mit seinem Wagen,
He drives his car,

gehen

geht ins Büro
walks into his office

schreiben

und schreibt einen Brief.
and writes a letter.

sprechen

Er spricht am Telefon,
He talks on the telephone,

erzählen

erzählt Nomen von einem Raubüberfall
tells Noun about a robbery

laufen

und läuft hinaus zu seinem Wagen.
and runs out to his car.

schauen

Er schaut sich ein Fenster an,
He looks at a window,

sehen

sieht einen Fußstapfen
sees a footprint

suchen

und sucht den Einbrecher.
and searches for the burglar.

verfolgen

Verb verfolgt den Einbrecher,
Verb chases the burglar,

fangen

fängt ihn
catches him

in ein Handgemenge geraten

und sie geraten in ein Handgemenge.
and they fight.

treten

Der Einbrecher tritt Verb,
The burglar kicks Verb,

schlagen

Verb schlägt den Einbrecher,
Verb hits the burglar

fallen

und er fällt um.
and he falls down.

aufheben

Verb hebt ihn auf,
Verb picks him up,

nehmen

nimmt ihn zur Polizeiwache
takes him to the police station

einsperren

und sperrt ihn ein.
and locks him in.

Inspektor Nomen und der preisgekrönte Bulle
Inspector Noun and the prize bull

Drei dumme Diebe versuchen, einen preisgekrönten Bullen zu stehlen.
Durch welche Tore geht Inspektor Nomen, um sie zu ertappen?
Three silly robbers try to steal a prize bull. Which gates does Inspector Noun go through to catch them?

das Bauernhaus

die Scheune

die Vogelscheuche

das Heu

der Garten

die Baumstämme*

der Karren

der Bauer

Inspektor Nomen

die Bäuerin

die Schweine*

der Schweinestall

die Puter*

die Ferkel*

der Hahn

der Hühnerstall

die Hühner*

die Gänschen*

die Küken*

die Gänse*

der Landarbeiter

die Enten*

der Teich

das Stroh

die Entchen*

der Stall

die Schafe*   die Lämmer*

die Ziege

10

der Schuppen

der Obstgarten

der Anhänger

der Traktor

der Pflug

der Silo

der Aufzug

der Wassertrog

das Gehege

der Schäfer

die Kühe*

der Kuhstall

der Schäferhund

die Kälber*

der Esel

der Bulle

die Pferde*

das Fohlen

der Lastwagen

11

Inspektor Nomen und die Fabrikspione
Inspector Noun and the factory spies

die Fabrik

Nomen steht draußen vor einer Fabrik Wache. Er sieht, wie zwei Spione herauslaufen.
Noun is on watch outside a factory. He sees two spies run out.

die Straße

Er folgt ihnen die Straße hinunter,
He follows them down the street,

das Tor

durch das Tor hindurch
through the gates

der Park

und in den Park hinein.
and into the park.

der See

Er läuft an dem See,
He walks past the lake,

die Schaukeln*

an den Schaukeln
the swings

die Marschkapelle

und an der Marschkapelle vorbei.
and the band.

die Schule

Die Spione sind bei einer Schule.
The spies are near a school.

das Gitter

Nomen blickt durch das Gitter
Noun looks through some railings

der Schulhof

und sieht sie auf dem Schulhof.
and sees them in the playground.

die Kirche

Er verfolgt sie an der Kirche vorbei,
He chases them past the church,

das Kino

um das Kino herum
round the cinema

das Hotel

und in das Hotel hinein.
and into a hotel.

das Café

Er findet die Spione in einem Café.
He finds the spies at a café.

die Ampel

Dann gehen sie zu der Ampel
Off they go to the traffic lights

der Fußgängerübergang

und überqueren die Straße an dem
and walk across the crossing. **Fußgängerübergang.**

die Bushaltestelle

Sie warten an einer Bushaltestelle.
They wait at a bus stop.

der Laternenpfahl

Nomen läuft hinter einen Laternenpfahl und versteckt sich hinter einer
Noun runs round a street lamp

die Statue

and hides behind a statue. **Statue.**

der Bus

Die Spione verpassen den Bus
The spies miss the bus

das Krankenhaus

und gehen zu Fuß weiter an dem Krankenhaus
and walk on past the hospital

das Loch

und an einem Loch in der
and a hole in the road. **Straße vorbei.**

der Preßlufthammer

Sie sehen dem Mann mit einem Preßlufthammer zu,
They watch the man with a drill,

der Bagger

werfen einen Blick auf einen Bagger
look at a digger

die Walze

und eine Walze.
and a roller.

die Röhren*

Sie springen über einige Röhren
They jump over some pipes

die Ziegelsteine*

und Ziegelsteine.
and some bricks.

der Polizist

Da sehen sie Nomen mit einem Polizisten.
Then they see Noun with a policeman.

das Büro

Sie rennen in ein Büro,
They hurry into an office,

das Treppenhaus

das Treppenhaus hinauf
up the stairs

die Feuerleiter

und auf die Feuerleiter.
and on to the fire escape.

das Dach

Nomen verfolgt sie bis auf das Dach,
Noun chases them on to the roof,

der Fahnenmast

um einen Fahnenmast herum
round a flag pole   and at last traps them by a chimney.

der Schornstein

und erwischt sie schließlich bei
einem Schornstein.

Inspektor Nomen fliegt mit einer Düsenmaschine
Inspector Noun goes flying

FLUGHAFEN

Inspektor Nomen fährt zum Flughafen. Er ist auf der Suche nach einem Schmuggler.
Inspector Noun drives to the airport. He is looking for a smuggler.

die Flugkarte

Er zeigt seine Flugkarte vor.
His ticket is checked.

der Zoll

Er geht durch den Zoll
He goes through the customs

der Pass

und läßt seinen Paß abstempeln.
and has his passport stamped.

die Abflughalle

Er wartet in die Abflughalle.
He waits in the departure lounge.

die Karte

Er bekommt seine Bordkarte.
He is given his boarding pass.

die Passagiere*

Er sieht sich die anderen Passagiere an.
He looks at the other passengers.

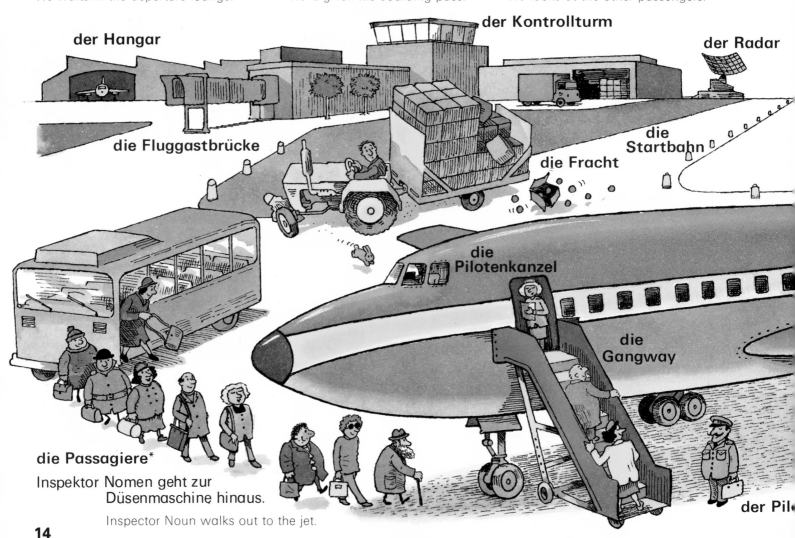

der Hangar

der Kontrollturm

der Radar

die Fluggastbrücke

die Startbahn

die Fracht

die Pilotenkanzel

die Gangway

die Passagiere*

Inspektor Nomen geht zur Düsenmaschine hinaus.
Inspector Noun walks out to the jet.

der Pil

das Flugzeug

Er geht durch das Flugzeug
He walks down the plane

der Sitz

bis zu seinem Sitz.
and finds his seat.

der Sicherheitsgurt

Er befestigt seinen Sicherheitsgurt.
He fastens his safety belt.

die Startbahn

Die Düsenmaschine rollt über die Startbahn und erhebt sich in die Luft.
The jet speeds down the runway

die Luft

and takes off into the air.

die Pilotenkanzel

Nomen geht in die Pilotenkanzel.
Noun goes to the flight deck.

der Pilot

Er spricht mit dem Piloten,
He talks to the pilot,

das Instrumentenbrett

wirft einen Blick auf das Instrumentenbrett
looks at the controls

der Gang

und geht wieder zurück den Gang entlang.
and walks down the gangway.

die Goldbarren*

Er sieht die Goldbarren, daraufhin flüstert er der Stewardess etwas ins Ohr
He sees the gold bars, so he whispers to the stewardess

die Stewardess

der Schmuggler

und verhaftet den Schmuggler.
and arrests the smuggler.

das Heck

der Tankwagen

die Tragfläche

das Düsentriebwerk

der Gepäckwagen

das Fahrgestell

die Stewardess

der Koffer

Inspektor Nomen und der Kostümverleih

Inspector Noun and the disguise shop

Nomen und sein Assistent gehen zu einem Kostümverleih. Wieviele Kostüme probieren sie an?

Noun and his assistant go to a shop disguise. How many disguises do they try on?

die Stiefel*

die Schuhe*

die Pantoffeln*

die Hüte*

die Kappen*

die Socken*

die Schlipse*

die Hosen*

die Kilts*

die Hemden*

die Jeans*

die Mäntel*

die Pullover*

die Handschuhe*

die Anoraks*

die Latzhosen*

die Anzüge*

die Regenmäntel*

die Perücken*

die falschen Nasen*

die Schlafanzüge*

die Uniformen*

die Bärte

die Schnurrbärte*

die Morgenmäntel*

die Shorts*

die T-shirts*

die Stiefel*

die Schuhe*

die Hüte*

die Handschuhe*

die Pantoffeln*

die Röcke*

die Kleider*

die Blusen*

die Handtaschen*

die Mäntel*

die Strumpfhosen*

die Strickjacken*

die Umhänge*

die Schals*

die Nachthemden*

die Morgenmäntel*

die Taschentücher*

die Pelzmäntel*

die Sonnenbrillen*

das Make-up

die Perücken*

der Schmuck

die Uniformen*

die Einkaufstaschen*

die Schürzen*

Inspektor Nomen und die Supermarktbande
Inspector Noun and the supermarket gang

Nomen geht zum Supermarkt. Er ist auf der Suche nach Lebensmitteldieben.
Noun goes to the supermarket. He is looking for some food robbers.

das Brot

Er geht am Brot
He walks past the bread

die Butter

und an der Butter vorbei
and the butter

der Käse

und sieht sich den Käse an.
and looks at the cheese.

die Milch

Er geht an der Milch
He goes past the milk

der Joghurt

und am Joghurt vorbei
and the yoghurt

die Eier*

und läßt einige Eier fallen.
and drops some eggs.

der Schinken

Er sieht sich den Schinken
Noun looks at the ham

der Speck

und den Speck an
and the bacon

der Fisch

und kriecht am Fisch vorbei.
and crawls past the fish.

das Mehl

Er blickt hinter das Mehl
He peers round the flour

der Zucker

und den Zucker
and the sugar

die Schokolade

und die Schokolade.
and the chocolate.

der Honig

Er steht beim Honig,
He stands by the honey,

die Marmelade

schaut sich die Marmelade an
looks at the jam

die Süßigkeiten*

und sucht sich ein paar Süßigkeiten aus.
and chooses some sweets.

die Kuchen*

Er läuft an den Kuchen
He runs past the cakes

die Plätzchen*

und Plätzchen vorbei
and the biscuits

die Brötchen*

und macht einen großen Schritt über die Brötchen.
and steps over the bread rolls.

die Dosen*

Er stößt Dosen
He knocks over tins

die Flaschen*

und Flaschen
and bottles

die Gläser*

und Gläser um.
and jars.

die Gefriertruhe

Er ruht sich bei der Gefriertruhe aus,
He rests by the freezer,

der Korb

tritt mit dem Fuß gegen einen Korb
kicks over a basket

die Kartons*

und einige Kartons.
and some boxes.

das Fleisch

Nomen findet etwas Fleisch,
Noun finds some meat,

das Hühnchen

ein Hühnchen
a chicken

die Würstchen*

und mehrere Würstchen.
and some sausages.

die Kasse

Er läuft an den Kassen vorbei,
He runs past the cash desk,

die Einkaufstaschen*

springt über ein paar Einkaufstaschen
jumps over some bags

die Säcke*

und über einige Säcke.
and some sacks.

die Diebe*

Dann erwischt er die Diebe.
Then he catches the robbers.

der Einkaufswagen

Er lädt sie in einen Einkaufswagen
He puts them in a trolley

das Hundegefängnis

und bringt sie ins Hundegefängnis.
and takes them to the dog prison.

19

Detektiv Präposition und das Gespensterschloß
Detective Preposition and the haunted castle

Detektiv Präposition geht zu dem Schloß. Dort haben Gauner einen Schatz versteckt.
Detective Preposition goes to the castle. Crooks have hidden some treasure there.

an

Er kommt am Wassergraben an,
He arrives at the moat,

über

geht über die Zugbrücke
walks over the drawbridge

unter

und unter dem Torbogen hindurch.
and goes under the gatehouse.

unter

Er schaut unter einen Stein,
He looks under a stone,

mit

sucht mit seiner Taschenlampe nach dem Schatz
searches for the treasure with his torch

zwischen

und leuchtet zwischen zwei Kanonen.
and shines it between two cannons.

bei

Als er bei einer Säule stehen bleibt,
As he stops near a pillar,

in der Nähe

hört er Schritte in der Nähe
he hears the sound of footsteps

in

und schaut in einen Raum.
and looks into a room.

hinter

Ein Gespenst erscheint hinter ihm,
A ghost appears behind him

vor

und dann steht es vor ihm.
and then stands in front of him.

auf . . . zu

Er läuft auf die Treppe zu.
He runs towards the stairs.

hinunter

Er springt schnell hinunter,
He jumps quickly down,

durch

fällt durch den Fußboden,
falls through the floor

auf

landet jedoch auf seinen Füßen.
but lands on his feet.

Detektiv Pronomen kommt zur Hilfe
Detective Pronoun to the rescue

Als Präposition nicht zurückkommt, fährt Detektiv Pronomen zu dem Gespensterschloß.
When Preposition does not come back, Detective Pronoun goes to the haunted castle.

sie

Sie geht durch das Tor,
She walks through the gate,

du

ruft „Wo bist du?"
shouts "Where are you?"

ihn

und sucht ihn.
and looks for him.

er

Dann sieht sie, daß er in das Verließ gefallen ist.
Then she sees he is in the dungeon.

mir

„Hilf mir bitte," sagt er.
"Please help me," he says.

ich

„Ich zieh' dich heraus," sagt sie.
"I will pull you out," she says.

wir

„Schnell, wir müssen uns verstecken.
"Quick, we must hide.

sie

Sie kommen hier herunter
They are coming down here

uns

und werden uns sehen."
and will see us."

ihn

„Wir haben ihn gefunden," sagen die Gauner.
"We have found it," say the crooks.

sie

Plötzlich sehen die Gauner sie,
Suddenly the crooks see her

sie

aber Pronomen verhaftet sie.
but Pronoun arrests them.

Inspektor Nomen und die Entführer
Inspector Noun and the kidnappers

Eines Nachts schlichen zehn Spione in ein Hotel, um einen berühmten Wissenschaftler zu entführen.
One night ten spies crept into a hotel to kidnap a famous scientist.

Als sie Inspektor Nomen kommen hörten, versteckten sie sich. Kannst du sie alle finden?
When they heard Inspector Noun coming, they hid. Can you find them all?

Inspektor Nomen verfolgt die Gauner
Inspector Noun chases the crooks

das Gefängnis

Zwei Gauner entkommen aus dem Gefängnis. Nomen läuft hinter ihnen her.
Two crooks escape from prison. Noun runs after them.

das Tandem

Sie fahren auf einem Tandem davon.
They ride away on a tandem.

das Fahrrad

Nomen verfolgt sie auf einem Fahrrad.
Noun chases them on a bicycle.

der Roller

Sie springen auf einen Roller.
They jump on a scooter.

die Rollschuhe*

Nomen folgt ihnen auf Rollschuhen.
Noun follows them on roller skates.

das Auto

Die Gauner stehlen ein Auto.
The crooks steal a car.

das Taxi

Nomen hält ein Taxi an.
Noun hires a taxi.

der Lastwagen

Sie entkommen in einem Lastwagen.
They drive off in a lorry.

der Lieferwagen

Nomen fährt mit einem Lieferwagen hinter ihnen her.
Noun follows them in a van.

das Flugzeug

Die Gauner heben in einem Flugzeug ab.
The crooks fly off in a plane.

der Hubschrauber

Nomen verfolgt sie in einem Hubschrauber.
Noun chases them in a helicopter.

der Fallschirm

Sie schweben an einem Fallschirm herab.
They come down by parachute.

der Zug

Sie steigen in einen Zug.
They catch a train.

das Motorboot

Sie stehlen ein Motorboot.
They steal a motor boat.

das Ruderboot

Sie springen in ein Ruderboot.
They jump into a rowing boat.

der Pferdetransporter

Sie stehlen einen Pferdetransporter.
They steal a horse box.

das Motorrad

Sie haben einen Unfall auf einem Motorrad.
They crash a motorbike.

der Ballon

Nomen landet in einem Ballon.
Noun lands in a balloon.

der Rennwagen

Nomen jagt sie in einem Rennwagen.
Noun drives after them in a racing car.

das Segelboot

Nomen folgt ihnen in einem Segelboot.
Noun follows in a sailing boat.

das Kanu

Nomen paddelt in einem Kanu hinter ihnen her.
Noun paddles after them in a canoe.

die Feuerwehr

Nomen wird von einer Feuerwehr mitgenommen.
Noun has a lift on a fire engine.

der Krankenwagen

Nomen fängt sie und transportiert sie in einem
Noun catches them and takes them away in an ambulance. Krankenwagen ab.

Die Schule für Verbdetektive
School for Verb Detectives

Hier sehen wir viele Verben in einer Schule für Detektive.
Kannst du die sechs Gauner entdecken, die sie beobachten?

Here are lots of Verbs at a school for detectives.
Can you find the six crooks watching them?

schieben

marschieren

ins Wasser springen

springen

schwimmen

tragen

Ball spielen

graben

ringen

schießen

kriechen

sich verstecken

Seilchen springen

lächeln

finden

ziehen

lachen

werfen

sitzen

reiten

26

rudern

Schlittschuh laufen

fliegen

schneiden

pusten

bauen

stehen

um die Wette laufen

malen

singen

ein Instrument spielen

dirigieren

warten

tanzen

denken

schaukeln

hüpfen

stricken

kochen

basteln

nähen

anhalten

27

Detektiv Adverb und der Fleischdieb
Detective Adverb and the meat thief

der Metzger   der Bäcker   die Blumen*

Eines Abends beobachtete Detektiv Adverb, wie ein Mann Fleisch stahl. Er sah folgendes.
One evening Detective Adverb saw a man stealing some meat. This is what he saw.

langsam

Ein Hund lief langsam daher
A dog was walking slowly along,

laut

und schnüffelte laut nach Essen.
sniffing loudly for food.

traurig

Dann setzte er sich traurig hin.
Then he sat down sadly.

plötzlich

bald

glücklich

Plötzlich stahl ein Mann etwas Fleisch, und der Hund hatte es bald aufgefressen. Er wackelte glücklich mit
A man suddenly grabbed some meat   and the dog soon ate it.   He wagged his tail happily.   dem Schwanz.

liebevoll

Der Mann streichelte den Hund liebevoll.
The man gently patted the dog

wütend

Der Metzger schimpfte wütend,
The butcher shouted angrily

schnell

und der Mann lief schnell davon.
and the man ran quickly away.

wild

Der Hund bellte wie wild.
The dog barked fiercely.

fast

Der Metzger erwischte ihn fast,
The butcher almost caught it

ebenfalls

aber er lief ebenfalls davon.
but it also ran away.

Detektiv Adjektivs Bericht
Detective Adjective's Report

Detektiv Adjektiv sah den Hund und den Mann. Sie beschreibt sie folgendermaßen:
Detective Adjective saw the dog and the man. This is her description of them.

dünn

Der Hund hatte einen dünnen Kopf,
The dog had a thin head,

spitz

spitze Ohren
pointed ears

braun

und braune Augen.
and brown eyes.

schwarz

Er hatte ein schwarzes Fell,
It had a black coat,

lang

einen langen Schwanz
a long tail

rot

und ein rotes Halsband.
and a red collar.

rund

Der Mann hatte ein rundes Gesicht,
The man had a round face,

lockig

lockige Haare
curly hair

grau

und einen grauen Bart.
and a grey beard.

grün

Er trug einen grünen Hut,
He wore a green hat,

alt

einen alten Mantel
an old coat

weiß

und ein weißes Hemd.
and a white shirt.

blau

Er trug eine blaue Hose,
He had blue trousers,

gelb

gelbe Socken
yellow socks

groß

und große Stiefel.
and big boots.

Inspektor Nomen und die Schmuggler
Inspector Noun and the smugglers

der Tanker

der Schlepper

das U-Boot

das Fischerboot

der Kran

das Luftkissen-
fahrzeug

das Frachtschiff

Inspektor Nomen lauert Schmugglern auf. Er will herausfinden, wo ihr Versteck ist.
Inspector Noun is waiting for some smugglers. He wants to find their hide-out.

das Motorboot

Er sieht ein Motorboot
He sees a motor boat

die Schmuggler*

und beobachtet die Schmuggler.
and watches the smugglers.

der Strand

Er folgt ihnen den Strand entlang.
He follows them along the beach.

die Sandburg

Sie gehen an einer Sandburg vorbei,
They walk past a sandcastle,

der Eimer

treten gegen einen Eimer
kick over a bucket

der Sonnenschirm

und stoßen einen Sonnenschirm um.
and knock down an umbrella.

der Spaten

Einer tritt auf einen Spaten,
One steps on a spade,

der Ball

ein anderer gegen einen Ball.
another kicks a ball.

das Picknick

Die Schmuggler legen eine
The smugglers stop for a picnic. Picknickspause ein.

das Wrack

die Hafenmauer

das Tragflächenboot

der Wasserskiläufer

die Autofähre

die Boje

die Kisten*

das Lagerhaus

die Kieselsteine*

Nomen sitzt auf den Kieselsteinen.
Noun sits on the pebbles.

der Krebs

Er hebt einen Krebs auf
He picks up a crab

der Felsentümpel

und setzt ihn in einen Felsentümpel.
and puts it into a rock pool.

die Felsen*

Er folgt den Männern bis zu den Felsen,
He follows the men to the rocks,

der Seetang

rutscht auf etwas Seetang aus
slips on some seaweed

der Leuchtturm

und erreicht den Leuchtturm.
and reaches the lighthouse.

die Klippe

Er klettert auf die Klippe,
He climbs up the cliff,

der Tunnel

kriecht in einen Tunnel
crawls into a tunnel

die Höhle

und findet das Versteck der Schmuggler in einer Höhle.
and finds the smugglers' hide-out in a cave.

Inspektor Nomen in Gefahr
Inspector Noun in danger

Nomen findet die Schmuggler in ihrer Höhle. Aber sie bemerken, daß er allein ist und machen sich daran, **ihn zu verfolgen.**
Noun finds the smugglers in their cave. But they see he is alone and start to chase him.

die Straße

Er rennt weg eine Straße hinunter,
He runs away along a road,

die Brücke

überquert eine Brücke
crosses over a bridge

die Kreuzung

und erreicht eine Kreuzung.
and reaches a crossroads.

der Wegweiser

Nomen bleibt stehen, um einen Wegweiser zu lesen,
Noun stops to read a sign post,

der Pfad

läuft weiter einen Pfad hinab
runs on down a path

die Hecke

und kriecht durch eine Hecke.
and crawls through a hedge.

die Bäume*

Er läuft auf ein paar Bäume zu.
He runs towards some trees.

der Fluß

Dann kommt er an einen Fluß
Then he comes to a river

das Floß

und paddelt auf einem Floß zum anderen Ufer.
and paddles across on a raft.

der Wasserfall

Mit Mühe rettet er sich vor einem Wasserfall,
He just misses a waterfall,

der Hügel

eilt einen Hügel hinauf
hurries up a hill

der Zaun

und springt über einen Zaun.
and jumps over a fence.

der Kanal

Nomen bleibt an einem Kanal stehen,
Noun stops by a canal,

der Kahn

springt auf einen Kahn
leaps on to a barge

die Schleuse

und steigt an einer Schleuse wieder ab.
and jumps off again at a lock.

32

das Tor

Nomen klettert über ein Tor,
Noun climbs over a gate,

die Zelte*

rennt an ein paar Zelten vorbei
hurries past some tents

die Leine

und stolpert über eine Leine.
and trips over a rope.

der Wohnwagen

Er rennt weiter an einem Wohnwagen vorbei,
He runs past a caravan,

der Bach

erreicht einen Bach
reaches a stream

die Steine*

und balanciert über die Steine ans
and crosses over by the stepping stones. **andere Ufer.**

die Staumauer

Er eilt über eine Staumauer,
He dashes across a dam,

die Windmühle

an einer Windmühle vorbei
past a windmill

der Wald

und in einen Wald hinein.
and into a forest.

der Berg

Er klettert auf einen Berg,
He starts to climb a mountain,

die Seilbahn

fährt mit einer Seilbahn
then rides in a cable car

der Schnee

und tritt hinaus in den Schnee
and steps out into snow.

die Schier*

Er probiert ein Paar Schier an,
He tries on some skis,

der Schlitten

rodelt auf einem Schlitten den Hang hinunter
slides down on a toboggan

die Mauer

und klettert über eine Mauer.
and then climbs over a wall.

der Raum

Er läuft in einen dunklen Raum
Noun runs into a dark room

das Licht

und knipst das Licht an. Die Schmuggler sind ihm auf einer
and switches on the light. The smugglers are caught in a police station.

die Polizeiwache

Polizeiwache in **die Falle gegangen.**

Inspektor Nomen im Zoo

Inspector Noun at the zoo

Im Zoo ist der Löwe aus seinem Käfig ausgebrochen. Welchem Pfad folgt Nomen, um ihn zu finden?

At the zoo the lion has escaped from its cage. Which path does Noun go along to find it?

der Käfig

der Wärter

Inspektor Nomen

der Eisbär

die Schlangen*

der Elefant

das Kamel

die Seehunde*

das Kängeruh

der Tiger

die Giraffe

die Pinguine*

die Eule

die Strauße*

die Flamingos*

die Krokodile*

Inspektor Nomen sucht nach Anhaltspunkten
Inspector Noun looks for clues

Nomen öffnet die Tür zu seinem Büro. „Hier war jemand," denkt er und macht sich auf
  die Suche nach Anhaltspunkten.
Noun opens the door of his office. "Someone has been in here," he thinks and looks for clues.

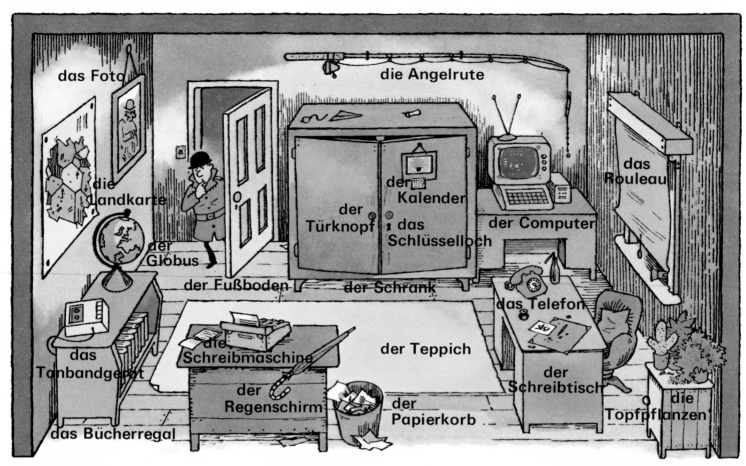

der Fußboden

Er betrachtet den Fußboden,
He looks at the floor,

die Schublade

entdeckt·eine offene Schublade
finds an open drawer

die Armbanduhr

und hebt eine Armbanduhr auf.
and picks up a watch.

der Schlüssel

Er findet einen Schlüssel
He finds a key

das Taschentuch

und ein Taschentuch
and a handkerchief

die Taschenlampe

und eine Taschenlampe.
and a torch.

der Füllfederhalter

die Briefmarke

der Briefumschlag

Irgendjemand hat seinen Füllfederhalter benutzt, eine Briefmarke gestohlen und einen Briefumschlag geöffnet.
Someone has used his pen,   stolen a stamp   and opened an envelope.

das Notizbuch

Jemand hat sein Notizbuch gelesen,
Someone has read his notebook,

der Computer

mit seinem Computer gespielt
played with his computer

der Taschenrechner

und seinen Taschenrechner fallen lassen.
and dropped his calculator.

der Bleistift

Jemand hat seinen Bleistift durchgebrochen,
Someone has broken his pencil,

das Getränk

sein Getränk ausgetrunken
finished his drink

das Butterbrot

und in sein Butterbrot gebissen.
and eaten his sandwich.

der Hammer
die Untertassen*
die Tassen*
die Teller*
die Streichhölzer*
die Lupe
der Feldstecher
die Schere
die Messer*
die Gabeln*
die Löffel*
der Fotoapparat
die Handschellen*
der Bindfaden
der Pinsel
die Gläser*
die Pfeife
der Krug
die Farbe
der Wecker
die Nägel*
das Geld
das Taschenmesser
die Säge
der Verbandskasten
die Sicherheitsnadeln*
die Verbände*
der Schallplattenspieler
die Schallplatten*
die Papiere*
die Bücher*
das Schwert
der Schraubenzieher
die Axt

Dann sieht er in seinen Schrank und findet den Einbrecher.
Then he looks in his cupboard and finds the burglar.

Inspektor Nomen fängt einen Weltraumspion

Inspector Noun catches a space spy

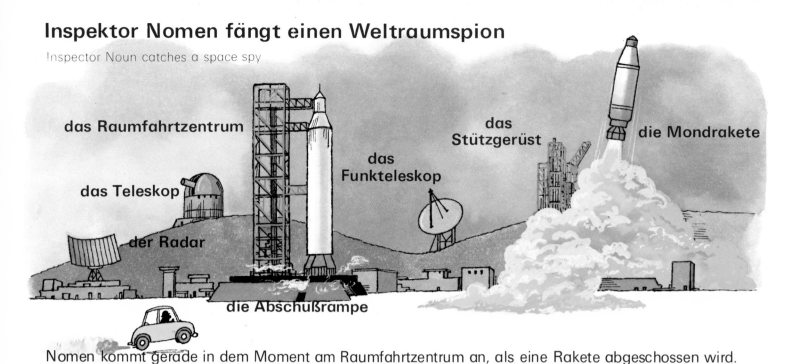

das Raumfahrtzentrum

das Stützgerüst

die Mondrakete

das Funkteleskop

das Teleskop

der Radar

die Abschußrampe

Nomen kommt gerade in dem Moment am Raumfahrtzentrum an, als eine Rakete abgeschossen wird. Er weiß, daß ein Spion an Bord ist.

Noun reaches the space launch station just as a rocket blasts off. He knows there is a spy on board.

der Raumanzug

Er zieht einen Raumanzug an
He puts on a space suit,

die Astronauten*

und trifft zwei Astronauten,
meets two astronauts

die Abschußrampe

die ihn zur Abschußrampe bringen.
and is taken to the launch pad.

das Raumschiff

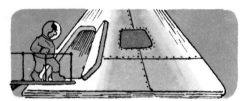

Er steigt in das Raumschiff,
He goes into the space craft,

die Liege

legt sich auf eine Liege,
lies on a couch

die Rakete

und die Rakete hebt ab.
and the rocket takes off.

die Erde

Er sieht die Erde unter sich
He sees the earth below

die Sonne

und blickt auf die Sonne
and looks at the sun

die Sterne*

und die Sterne.
and the stars.

die Raumfähre

Er schießt an einer Raumfähre,
He whizzes past a space shuttle,

der Satellit

einem Satelliten
a satellite

die Raumstation

und einer Raumstation vorbei.
and a space station.

das Mondfahrzeug

die Mondlandefähre

Nomen landet auf dem Mond. Die andere Rakete ist schon da.
Noun lands on the moon. The other rocket is there.

das Mondfahrzeug

Er fährt mit einem Mondfahrzeug,
He rides on a moon buggy, sees footprints

der Mondstaub

bemerkt Fußstapfen im Mondstaub
in the moon dust and catches the spy by a moon rock.

das Mondgestein

und fängt den Spion hinter einem Brocken Mondgestein.

der Weltraum

Er fliegt zurück in den Weltraum.
He takes off into space again.

der Meteor

Ein Meteor trifft die Raumkapsel.
The module is hit by a meteor

der Spaziergang im All

Nomen macht einen Spaziergang im All.
Noun goes for a space walk.

die Antenne

Er repariert die Antenne.
He mends an antenna.

die Erdumlaufbahn

Die Raumkapsel kehrt in die Erdumlaufbahn zurück
The module goes into orbit

das Meer

und landet im Meer.
and they splash down in the sea.

die Einstiegsluke

Sie klettern aus der Einstiegsluke.
They climb out of the nose cone.

die Froschmänner*

Froschmänner stehen bereit, um ihnen zu helfen.
Frogmen are there to help them.

die Mission

Die Mission ist zu einem sicheren Ende gekommen.
The mission is safely over.

INDEX

On this page is the start of the alphabetical list of all the single words on the pictures in this book. The German word comes first, then there is its pronunciation in *italics*, followed by the English translation.

Although some German words look like English ones, they are not pronounced in the same way. And some letters have different sounds. In German, w sounds like English v, v sounds like f, z like ts, and j like y in young. There are also some sounds in German which are quite unlike sounds in English.

The pronunciation is a guide to help you say the words correctly. They may look funny or strange. Just read them as if they are English words, except for these special rules:

ah	—is said like s in *farther*
a	—is said like *ah* but shorter
ow	—is like *ow* in cow
ew	—is different from any sound in English. To make it say *ee* with your lips rounded
ee	—is like *ee* in *week*
ay	—is like *ay* in *day*
y	—is like y in *try*, except when it comes before a vowel. Then it sounds like y in *young*
g	—as g in *garden*
ch	—is said like *ch* in the Scottish word *loch*
kh	—is said like the h in *huge*
r	—is made at the back of your mouth and sounds a little like gargling
e(r)	—is like the e in the (not *thee*). When the r is in brackets (r), it is not said
u(r)	—is like i in *bird*. The r is not said
oo	—is a short vowel, like in *foot*
$\overline{oo}$	—is a long vowel, like in *food*

die Abschußrampe	*dee ap-shooss-rampe(r)*	launch pad
der Adler	*derr ahdler*	eagle
die Affen	*dee affen*	monkeys
alt	*alt*	old
die Ampel	*dee ampel*	traffic lights
an	*an*	at
die Ananas	*dee ananas*	pineapple
die Angelrute	*dee angel-rōōte(r)*	fishing rod
anhalten	*anhalten*	to stop
der Anhänger	*derr anhenger*	trailer
der Anker	*derr anker*	anchor
die Anoraks	*dee anoraks*	anoraks
die Antenne	*dee antenne(r)*	antenna
anziehen	*an-tsee-en*	to put on
die Anzüge	*dee an-tsewge(r)*	suits
der Apfel	*derr apfel*	apple
die Aprikosen	*dee aprikoazen*	apricots
die Armbanduhr	*dee arm-bant-ōōr*	watch
die Astronauten	*dee astro-nowten*	astronauts
auf	*owf*	on
auf . . . zu	*owf . . . . . tsoo*	towards
aufdrehen	*owf-drayen*	to turn on
der Aufenthalts- raum	*derr owfenthalts- rowm*	saloon
aufheben	*owf-hayben*	to pick up
aufwachen	*owf-vachen*	to wake up
der Aufzug	*derr owf-tsook*	elevator
ausziehen	*owss-tsee-en*	to take off
das Auto	*dass owto*	car
die Autofähre	*dee owto-fehre(r)*	car ferry
die Axt	*dee axt*	axe
das Baby	*dass baby*	baby
der Bach	*derr bach*	stream
der Bäcker	*derr becker*	baker

die Backöfen	*dee back-u(r)fen*	ovens
das Badezimmer	*dass bahde(r)-tsimmer*	bathroom
der Bagger	*derr bagger*	digger
bald	*balt*	soon
der Balkon	*derr balkoan*	balcony
der Ball	*derr ball*	ball
der Ballon	*derr balloan*	balloon
Ball spielen	*ball shpeelen*	to play ball
die Bananen	*dee bananen*	bananas
die Bären	*dee behren*	bears
basteln	*basteln*	to make
bauen	*bowen*	to build
der Bauer	*derr bower*	farmer
die Bäuerin	*dee boyerin*	farmer's wife
das Bauernhaus	*dass bowern-howss*	farmhouse
die Bäume	*dee boyme(r)*	trees
die Baumstämme	*dee bowm-shtemme(r)*	logs
bei	*bye*	by
der Berg	*derr berk*	mountain
das Bett	*dass bett*	bed
der Biber	*derr beeber*	beaver
das Bier	*dass beer*	beer
das Bild	*dass bilt*	picture
der Bindfaden	*derr bint-fahden*	string
die Birnen	*dee beernen*	pears
blau	*blow*	blue
der Bleistift	*derr blye-shtift*	pencil
die Blumen	*dee blōōmen*	flowers
der Blumenkohl	*derr blōōmen-koal*	cauliflower
die Blusen	*dee bloozen*	blouses
die Bohnen	*dee boanen*	beans
der Boiler	*derr boyler*	boiler
die Boje	*dee boa-ye(r)*	buoy
die Braptfanne	*dee braht-pfanne(r)*	frying pan
braun	*brown*	brown
die Briefmarke	*dee breef-marke(r)*	stamp

der Briefumschlag	*derr breef-oom-shlahk*	envelope
das Brot	*dass broat*	bread
die Brücke	*dee brewke(r)*	bridge
die Bücher	*dee bewkher*	books
das Bücherregal	*dass bewkher-raygal*	bookcase
der Büffel	*derr bewfel*	buffalo
der Bug	*derr bōōk*	bow (of ship)
die Bullaugen	*dee bool-owgen*	port holes
der Bulle	*derr boole(r)*	bull
das Büro	*dass bewro*	office
bürsten	*bewrsten*	to brush
der Bus	*derr booss*	bus
die Bushaltestelle	*dee boos-halte(r)-shtelle(r)*	bus stop
die Butter	*dee booter*	butter
das Butterbrot	*dass booter-broat*	sandwich
das Café	*dass kafay*	café
der Computer	*derr komputer*	computer
das Dach	*dass dach*	roof
das Deck	*dass dek*	deck
die Decke	*dee deke(r)*	blanket
denken	*denken*	to think
die Diamanten	*dee dee-amanten*	diamonds
der Dieb	*derr deep*	robber, thief
dirigieren	*dirigeeren*	to conduct
die Dosen	*dee doazen*	tins
du	*doo*	you
dünn	*dewn*	thin
durch	*doorch*	through
die Dusche	*dee dooshe(r)*	shower
die Düsenmaschine	*dee dewzen-masheene(r)*	jet
das Düsentriebwerk	*dass dewzen-treep-vairk*	engine
ebenfalls	*ayben-falls*	also
die Eier	*dee eyer*	eggs
der Eimer	*derr eymer*	bucket
die Einkaufstaschen	*dee eyne-kowfs-tashen*	shopping bags
der Einkaufswagen	*derr eyne-kowfs-vahgen*	shopping trolley
einsperren	*eyne-shperren*	to lock in
die Einstiegsluke	*dee eyne-shteeks-lōōke(r)*	nose cone
der Eisbär	*derr eyss-bair*	polar bear
der Elefant	*derr elefant*	elephant
der Empfang	*derr empfank*	reception
die Entchen	*dee entkhen*	ducklings
die Enten	*dee enten*	ducks
er	*err*	he
die Erbsen	*dee airpsen*	peas
die Erdbeeren	*dee airt-bairen*	strawberries
die Erde	*dee airde(r)*	earth
die Erdumlaufbahn	*dee aird-oom-lowf-bahn*	orbit
erzälen	*err-tsaylen*	to tell
der Esel	*derr ayzel*	donkey
essen	*essen*	to eat
die Fabrik	*dee fabreek*	factory
der Fahnenmast	*derr fahnenmast*	flag pole
fahren	*fahren*	to drive
das Fahrgestell	*dass fahr-geshtell*	wheels
das Fahrrad	*dass fahr-raht*	bicycle
fallen	*fallen*	to fall
fallen lassen	*fallen lassen*	to drop
das Fallreep	*dass fallreep*	gang plank
der Fallschirm	*derr fall-sheerm*	parachute
fangen	*fangen*	to catch
die Farbe	*dee farbe(r)*	paint
fast	*fast*	almost
der Feldstecher	*derr felt-shtekher*	binoculars
die Felsen	*dee felzen*	rocks
der Felsentümpel	*derr felzen-tewmpel*	rock pool
die Ferkel	*dee fairkel*	piglets
der Fernseher	*derr fern-zayer*	television
die Feuerleiter	*dee foyer-lyter*	fire escape
die Feuerwehr	*dee foyer-vair*	fire engine
finden	*finden*	to find
der Fisch	*derr fish*	fish
das Fischerboot	*dass fisher-boat*	fishing boat
die Flagge	*dee flagge(r)*	flag
die Flamingos	*dee flamingoaz*	flamingos
die Flaschen	*dee flashen*	bottles
das Fleisch	*dass flysh*	meat
fliegen	*fleegen*	to fly
das Floß	*dass floass*	raft
die Fluggastbrücke	*dee flōōk-gast-brewke(r)*	passenger bridge
der Flughafen	*derr flōōk-hahfen*	airport
die Flugkarte	*dee flōōk-karte(r)*	ticket
das Flugzeug	*dass flōōk-tsoyk*	plane
der Fluß	*derr flooss*	river
das Fohlen	*dass foalen*	foal
das Foto	*dass foto*	photograph
der Fotoapparat	*derr foto-apparaht*	camera
die Fracht	*dee fracht*	cargo
das Frachtschiff	*dass fracht-shiff*	cargo boat
die Frau	*dee frow*	woman
der Frisiertisch	*derr friseer-tish*	dressing table
die Froschmänner	*dee frosh-menner*	frogmen
der Füllfederhalter	*derr-fewl-fayder-halter*	pen
das Funkteleskop	*dass foonk-teleskoap*	radio telescope
der Fußboden	*derr fōōss-boaden*	floor
der Fußgängerübergang	*derr fōōss-genger-ewber-gank*	crossing
füttern	*fewtern*	to feed
die Gabeln	*dee gahbeln*	forks
der Gang	*derr gank*	gangway
die Gangway	*dee gangway*	steps
die Gänschen	*dee genss-khen*	goslings
die Gänse	*dee genze(r)*	geese
der Garten	*derr garten*	garden
das Gefängnis	*dass gefengnis*	prison
die Gefriertruhe	*dee gefreertrōō-e(r)*	freezer
das Gehege	*dass gehayge(r)*	yard
gehen	*gayen*	to walk
gelb	*gelp*	yellow
das Geld	*dass gelt*	money
das Gemüse	*dass gemewze(r)*	vegetables
der Gepäckwagen	*derr gepeck-vahgen*	baggage train
die Geschirrspülmaschine	*dass gesheer-shpewl-masheene(r)*	dishwasher

das Getränk	*dass getrenk*	a drink
die Giraffe	*dee giraffe(r)*	giraffe
das Gitter	*dass gitter*	railings
die Gläser	*dee glayzer*	glasses, jars
der Globus	*derr gloabooss*	globe
glücklich	*glewk-likh*	happily
die Goldbarren	*dee golt-barren*	gold bars
graben	*grahben*	to dig
grau	*grow*	grey
groß	*groass*	big
grün	*grewn*	green
die Hafenmauer	*dee hahfen-mower*	harbour wall
der Hahn	*derr hahn*	cockerel
die Halle	*dee halle(r)*	lounge
der Hammer	*derr hammer*	hammer
in ein Hand-gemenge geraten	*in eyne hant-gemenge(r) gerahten*	to fight
die Handschellen	*dee hant-shellen*	handcuffs
die Handschuhe	*dee hant-shoo-e(r)*	gloves
die Handtaschen	*dee hant-tashen*	handbags
das Handtuch	*dass hant-tooch*	towel
der Hangar	*derr hangar*	hangar
das Heck	*dass hek*	stern, tail
die Hecke	*dee heke(r)*	hedge
der Heizkörper	*derr hyts-ku(r)per*	radiator
die Hemden	*dee hemden*	shirts
das Heu	*dass hoy*	hay
die Himbeeren	*dee him-bairen*	raspberries
hinter	*hinter*	behind
hinunter	*hinoonter*	down
die Höhle	*dee hu(r)le(r)*	cave
der Honig	*derr hoanig*	honey
die Hosen	*dee hoazen*	trousers
das Hotel	*dass hotel*	hotel
der Hubschrauber	*derr hoop-shrowber*	helicopter
der Hügel	*derr hewgel*	hill
das Hühnchen	*dass hewn-khen*	chicken
die Hühner	*dee hewner*	hens
der Hühnerstall	*derr hewner-shtall*	hen house
hüpfen	*hewpfen*	to hop
die Hüte	*dee hewte(r)*	hats
ich	*ikh*	I
ihn	*een*	he, it
ihr	*eer*	her, it
in	*in*	into
in der Nähe	*in derr naye(r)*	near
Inspektor Nomen	*inspektor nomen*	Inspector Noun
das Instrumenten-brett	*dass instroomenten-brett*	controls
ein Instrument spielen	*eyne instroment shpeelen*	to play (an instrument)
die Jeans	*dee jeans*	jeans
der Joghurt	*derr yogoort*	yoghurt
die Jungen	*dee yoongen*	boys
die Kabine	*dee kabeene(r)*	cabin
der Käfig	*derr kayfik*	cage
der Kahn	*derr kahn*	barge
die Kälber	*dee kelber*	calves
der Kalender	*derr kalender*	calendar
das Kamel	*dass kamel*	camel
der Kamin	*derr kameen*	fireplace

der Kanal	*derr kanahl*	canal
das Kängeruh	*dass kengooroo*	kangaroo
das Kanu	*dass kanoo*	canoe
der Kapitän	*derr kapitayn*	captain
die Kappen	*dee kappen*	caps
der Karren	*derr karren*	cart
die Karte	*dee karte(r)*	pass
die Kartoffeln	*dee kartoffeln*	potatoes
die Kartons	*dee kartoanz*	boxes
der Käse	*derr kayze(r)*	cheese
die Kasse	*dee kasse(r)*	cash desk
der Kellner	*derr kellner*	waiter
die Kette	*dee kette(r)*	chain
die Kieselsteine	*dee keezel-shtyne(r)*	pebbles
die Kilts	*dee kilts*	kilts
das Kinderbett	*dass kinderbett*	cot
der Kinderwagen	*derr kinder-vahgen*	pram
das Kino	*dass keeno*	cinema
die Kirche	*dee keerkhe(r)*	church
die Kirschen	*dee keershen*	cherries
das Kissen	*dass kissen*	cushion
die Kisten	*dee kisten*	crates
die Kleider	*dee klyder*	dresses
der Kleiderschrank	*derr klyder-shrank*	wardrobe
die Klippe	*dee klippe(r)*	cliff
kochen	*kochen*	to cook
der Kochherd	*derr koch-hairt*	cooker
der Koffer	*derr koffer*	suitcase
die Kohle	*dee koale(r)*	coal
die Kohlköpfe	*dee koal-ku(r)pfe(r)*	cabbages
die Koje	*dee koa-ye(r)*	bunk
die Kommando-brücke	*dee kommando-brewke(r)*	bridge (of ship)
der Kontrollturm	*derr kontrol-toorm*	control tower
das Kopfkissen	*dass kopf-kissen*	pillow
der Korb	*derr korp*	basket
der Korridor	*derr korridor*	corridor
der Kran	*derr krahn*	crane
das Krankenhaus	*dass kranken-howss*	hospital
der Krankenwagen	*derr kranken-vahgen*	ambulance
der Krebs	*derr kreps*	crab
der Kreuzung	*derr kroytsoonk*	cross road
kriechen	*kreekhen*	to crawl
die Krokodile	*dee krokodeele(r)*	crocodiles
der Krug	*derr krook*	jug
die Küche	*dee kewkhe(r)*	kitchen
die Kuchen	*dee koochen*	cakes
der Küchenchef	*derr kewkhen-shef*	chef
die Kühe	*dee kewe(r)*	cows
der Kühlschrank	*derr kewl-shrank*	refrigerator
der Kuhstall	*derr koo-shtall*	cowshed
die Küken	*dee kewken*	chicks
lächeln	*lekheln*	to smile
lachen	*lachen*	to laugh
der Laderaum	*derr laderowm*	hold (of ship)
das Lagerhaus	*dass lager-howss*	warehouse
die Lämmer	*dee lemmer*	lambs
die Lampe	*dee lampe(r)*	lamp
der Landarbeiter	*derr lant-arbyter*	farm worker
die Landkarte	*dee lant-karte(r)*	map
lang	*lank*	long
langsam	*langzam*	slowly
der Lastwagen	*derr last-vahgen*	lorry
der Laternen-pfahl	*derr latairnen-pfahl*	lamp post
die Latzhosen	*dee lats-hoazen*	dungarees

German	Pronunciation	English
der Lauch	derr lowkh	leek
laufen	lowfen	to run
laut	lowt	loudly
die Leine	dee lyne(r)	rope
die Leiter	dee lyter	ladder
lesen	layzen	to read
der Leuchtturm	derr loykht-toorm	lighthouse
das Licht	dass likht	light
liebevoll	leebefoll	gently
der Lieferwagen	derr leefer-vahgen	van
die Liege	dee leege(r)	couch
der Liegestuhl	derr leege(r)-shtool	deckchair
der Lift	derr lift	lift
das Loch	dass loch	hole
lockig	lokik	curly
die Löffel	dee lu(r)fel	spoons
der Löwe	derr lu(r)ve(r)	lion
die Luft	dee looft	air
das Luftkissen-fahrzeug	dass looft-kissen-fahr-tsoyk	hovercraft
die Luke	dee looke(r)	hatch
die Lupe	dee loope(r)	magnifying glass
die Mädchen	dee meht-khen	girls
das Make-up	dass 'make-up'	make-up
malen	mahlen	paint
der Mann	derr mann	man
die Mannschafts-kabine	dee mann-shafts-kabeene(r)	crew's cabin
die Mäntel	dee mentel	coats
der Markt	derr markt	market
die Marmelade	dee marmelahde(r)	jam
marschieren	marsheeren	march
die Marschkapelle	dee marsh-kapelle(r)	band
der Maschinen-raum	derr masheenen-rowm	engine room
der Maschinist	derr masheenist	engineer
der Mast	derr mast	mast
der Matrose	derr matroaze(r)	sailor
die Mauer	dee mower	wall
das Meer	dass mair	sea
das Mehl	dass mayl	flour
die Melone	dee meloane(r)	melon
die Messer	dee messer	knives
der Meteor	derr may-tee-oar	meteor
der Metzger	derr metsger	butcher
die Milch	dee milkh	milk
mir	meer	me, my
die Mission	dee miss-ee-oan	mission
mit	mit	with
die Möhren	dee muren	carrots
das Mondfahrzeug	dass moant-fahr-tsoyk	moon buggy
das Mondgestein	dass moant-geshtyne	moon rock
die Mond-landefähre	dee moant-landefehre(r)	lunar module
die Mondrakete	dee moant-rakayte(r)	moon rocket
der Mondstaub	derr moant-shtowp	moon dust
die Morgenmäntel	dee morgen-mantel	dressing gowns
das Motorboot	dass motoar-boat	motor boat
das Motorrad	dass motoar-raht	motor bike
die Möwe	dee mu(r)ve(r)	gull
die Nachthemden	dee nacht-hemden	nightdresses
die Nägel	dee naygel	nails
nähen	nayen	to sew
die falschen Nasen	dee falshen nahzen	false noses
die Nashörner	dee nahz-hurner	rhinoceroses
nehmen	naymen	to take
die Nilpferde	dee neel-pfairt	hippo-potamuses
das Notizbuch	dass notits-booch	notebook
das Obst	dass oapst	fruit
der Obstgarten	derr oapst-garten	orchard
öffnen	u(r)fnen	to open
die Orangen	dee oronjen	oranges
die Pampelmuse	dee pampelmooze(r)	grapefruit
der Panda	derr panda	panda
die Pantoffeln	dee pantoffeln	slippers
der Papagei	derr papagye	parrot
die Papiere	dee papeere(r)	papers
der Papierkorb	derr papeer-korp	wastepaper basket
der Park	derr park	park
der Pass	derr pass	passport
die Passagiere	dee passajeere(r)	passengers
der Pelikan	der pelikahn	pelican
die Pelzmäntel	dee pelts-mentel	fur coats
die Perücken	dee perewken	wigs
der Pfad	derr pfaht	path
die Pfeife	dee pfyfe(r)	whistle
die Pferde	dee pfairde(r)	horses
der Pferde-transporter	derr pfairde(r)-transporter	horse box
der Pfirsich	derr pfeerzikh	peach
die Pflaumen	dee pflowmen	plums
der Pflug	derr pflook	plough
das Picknick	dass piknik	picnic
der Pilot	derr peeloat	pilot
die Pilotenkanzel	dee peeloaten-kantsel	flight deck
die Pilze	dee piltse(r)	mushrooms
die Pinguine	dee pingoo-eene(r)	penguins
der Pinsel	derr pinzel	brush
die Plätzchen	dee plets-khen	biscuits
plötzlich	plu(r)ts-likh	suddenly
die Polizeiwache	dee politsye-vache(r)	police station
der Polizist	derr politsist	policeman
der Preßluft-hammer	derr press-looft-hammer	drill
die Pullover	dee poolover	jerseys
pusten	poosten	to blow
die Puter	dee pooter	turkeys
putzen	pootsen	to clean
der Radar	derr raydar	radar
die Radieschen	dee radeez-khen	radishes
die Rakete	dee rakayte(r)	rocket
der Raum	derr rowm	room
der Raumanzug	derr rowm-antsook	space suit
die Raumfähre	dee rowm-fehre(r)	space shuttle
das Raumfahrt-zentrum	dass rowm-fahrt-tsentroom	space launch station
die Raumkapsel	dee rowm-kapsel	command module
das Raumschiff	dass rowm-schiff	space craft
die Raumstation	dee rowm-shtatsee-oan	space station
die Regale	dee raygahle(r)	shelves
die Regenmäntel	dee raygen-mentel	raincoats

German	Pronunciation	English
der Regenschirm	derr raygen-sheerm	umbrella
reiben	ryben	to rub
reiten	ryten	to ride
die Reling	dee raylink	railings
der Rennwagen	derr renn-vahgen	racing car
das Rentier	dass rehn-teer	reindeer
die Rettungsboote	dee rettoongz-boate(r)	lifeboats
ringen	ringen	to wrestle
die Röcke	dee ru(r)ke(r)	skirts
die Röhren	dee ruren	pipes
der Roller	derr roller	scooter
die Rollschuhe	dee roll-shoo-en	roller skates
der Rosenkohl	derr roazen-koal	brussel sprouts
rot	roat	red
die Rote Bete	dee roate(r) bayte(r)	beetroot
das Rouleau	dass rooloa	blind
die Rüben	dee rewben	turnips
das Ruderboot	dass rooder-boat	rowing boat
rudern	roodern	to row
rund	roont	round
rutschen	rootshen	to slide
die Säcke	dee zeke(r)	sacks
die Säge	dee zehge(r)	saw
der Salat	derr zalaht	lettuce
die Sandburg	dee zant-boork	sand castle
der Satellit	derr zatelleet	satellite
die Schafe	dee shahfe(r)	sheep
der Schäfer	derr shayfer	shepherd
der Schäferhund	derr shayfer-hoont	sheepdog
die Schallplatten	dee shall-platten	records
der Schallplatten- spieler	der shall-platten- shpeeler	record player
die Schals	dee shahlz	scarves
schauen	showen	to look
schaukeln	showkeln	to swing
die Schere	dee shaire(r)	scissors
die Scheune	dee shoyne(r)	barn
die Schier	dee shee-er	skis
schießen	sheessen	to push, to shoot
das Schiff	dass shiff	ship
die Schiffskatze	dee shiffs-katse(r)	ship's cat
die Schiffs- schraube	dee shiffs-shrowbe(r)	propellor
die Schildkröte	dee shilt-kru(r)te(r)	tortoise
der Schinken	derr shinken	ham
die Schlafanzüge	dee shlahf-antsewge(r)	pyjamas
schlafen	shlahfen	to sleep
das Schlafzimmer	dass shlahf-tsimmer	bedroom
schlagen	shlahgen	to hit
die Schlangen	dee shlangen	snakes
der Schlepper	derr shlepper	tug boat
die Schleuse	dee shloyze(r)	lock
schließen	shleessen	to close
die Schlipse	dee shlipse(r)	ties
der Schlitten	derr shlitten	toboggan
Schlittschuh laufen	shlitt-shoolowfen	to skate
der Schlüssel	derr shlewssel	key
das Schlüsselloch	dass shlewssel-loch	keyhole
der Schmuck	derr shmook	jewellery
der Schmuggler	derr shmoogler	smuggler
der Schnee	derr shnay	snow
schneiden	shnyden	to cut
schnell	shnell	quickly
die Schnurrbärte	dee shnoor-bairte(r)	moustaches
die Schokolade	dee shokolahde(r)	chocolate
der Schornstein	derr shorn-shtyne	chimney, funnel
der Schrank	derr shrank	cupboard
der Schrauben- zieher	derr shrowben-tsee-er	screwdriver
schreiben	shryben	to write
die Schreib- maschine	dee shryp-masheene(r)	typewriter
der Schreibtisch	derr shryp-tish	desk
die Schublade	dee shoob-lahde(r)	drawer
die Schuhe	dee shoo-e(r)	shoes
die Schule	dee shoole(r)	school
der Schulhof	derr shool-hoaf	playground
der Schuppen	derr shoopen	shed
die Schürze	dee shewrtse(r)	apron
schwarz	shvarts	black
die Schweine	dee shvyne(r)	pigs
der Schweinestall	derr shvyne(r)-shtall	pigsty
das Schwert	dass shvairt	sword
schwimmen	shvimmen	to swim
der See	derr zay	lake
die Seehunde	dee zayhoonde(r)	seals
der Seetang	derr zaytank	sea weed
das Segelboot	dass zaygel-boat	sailing boat
sehen	zayen	to see
die Seife	dee zyfe(r)	soap
die Seilbahn	dee zyle-bahn	cable car
Seilchen springen	zyle-khen shpringen	to skip
die Sellerie	dee selleree	celery
der Sessel	derr zessel	arm chair
die Shorts	dee shorts	shorts
der Sicherheits- gurt	derr zikher-hyts-goort	safety belt
die Sicherheits- nadeln	dee zikher-hyts-nadeln	safety pins
sie	zee	her, she, them, they
der Silo	derr zeelo	silo
singen	zingen	to sing
der Sitz	derr zits	seat
sitzen	zitsen	to sit
die Socken	dee zoken	socks
die Sonne	dee zonne(r)	sun
die Sonnenbrillen	dee zonnen-brillen	sun glasses
der Sonnenschirm	derr zonnen-sheerm	beach umbrella, sunshade
der Spaten	derr shpahten	spade
der Spaziergang im All	derr shpatseer-gank im all	space walk
der Speck	derr shpek	bacon
der Speisesaal	derr shpyze(r)-zahl	dining room
der Spiegel	derr shpeegel	mirror
spitz	shpits	pointed
sprechen	shprekhen	to talk
springen	shpringen	to jump
der Spülstein	derr shpewl-shtyne	sink
das Stachel- schwein	dass shtachel-shvyne	porcupine
der Stall	derr shtall	stable
die Startbahn	dee shtart-bahn	runway
die Statue	dee shtahtoo-e(r)	statue
der Staubsauger	derr shtowp-zowger	vacuum cleaner
die Staumauer	dee shtow-mower	dam

German	Pronunciation	English
stehen	shtayen	to stand
steigen	shtygen	to climb
die Steine	dee shtyne(r)	stepping stones
die Sterne	dee shtairne(r)	stars
das Steuerruder	dass shtoyer-rooder	rudder
die Stewardess	dee stewardess	stewardess
die Stiefel	dee shteefel	boots
der Strand	der shtrant	beach
die Straße	dee shtrahsse(r)	road, street
die Strauße	dee shtrowsse(r)	ostriches
die Streichhölzer	dee shtrykh-hu(r)ltser	matches
stricken	shtriken	to knit
die Strickjacken	dee shtrik-yaken	cardigans
das Stroh	dass shtroa	straw
die Strumpfhosen	dee shtroompf-hoazen	tights
der Stuhl	derr shtool	chair
das Stützgerüst	dass shtewts-gerewst	gantry
suchen	zoochen	to search
der Supermarkt	derr zooper-markt	supermarket
die Süßigkeiten	dee zewssig-kyten	sweets
das Tandem	dass tandem	tandem
der Tanker	derr tanker	tanker
der Tankwagen	derr tank-vahgen	fuel tanker
tanzen	tantsen	to dance
die Taschen	dee tashen	pockets
die Taschenlampe	dee tashenlampe(r)	torch
das Taschenmesser	dass tashenmesser	penknife
der Taschenrechner	derr tashen-rekhner	calculator
die Taschentücher	dee tashen-tewkher	handkerchiefs
die Tassen	dee tassen	cups
das Taxi	dass taxi	taxi
der Teich	derr tykh	pond
das Telefon	dass telefoan	telephone
das Teleskop	dass teleskoap	telescope
die Teller	dee teller	plates
der Teppich	derr teppikh	carpet
der Tiger	derr teeger	tiger
der Tisch	derr tish	table
die Toilette	dee toilette(r)	toilet
die Tomate	dee tomate(r)	tomato
das Tonbandgerät	dass toanbant-gerayt	tape recorder
die Töpfe	dee tu(r)pfe(r)	saucepans
die Topfpflanzen	dee topf-pflentsen	plants
das Tor	dass tor	gate
tragen	trahgen	to carry
die Tragfläche	dee trahk-flekhe(r)	wing
das Tragflächenboot	dass trahk-flekhen-boat	hydrofoil
der Traktor	derr traktor	tractor
die Trauben	dee trowben	grapes
traurig	trowrik	sadly
die Treppe	dee treppe(r)	stairs
der Treppenabsatz	derr treppen-apzats	landing
das Treppenhaus	dass treppen-howss	stairwell
treten	trayten	to kick
trinken	trinken	to drink
die T-shirts	dee tee-shirts	tee-shirts
der Tukan	derr tookahn	toucan
der Tunnel	derr toonel	tunnel
der Türknopf	derr tewrn-knopf	door handle
über	ewber	over
das U-Boot	dass oo-boat	submarine
die Uhr	dee oor	clock
die Umhänge	dee oom-henge(r)	cloaks
die Uniformen	dee ooniformen	uniforms
unter	oonter	under
die Untertassen	dee oontertassen	saucers
die Verbände	dee ferbende(r)	bandages
der Verbandskasten	derr ferbants-kasten	first-aid kit
verfolgen	ferfolgen	to chase
sich verstecken	zikh fershteken	to hide
die Vogelscheuche	dee foagel-shoykhe(r)	scarecrow
vor	for	in front of
die Vorhänge	dee for-henge(r)	curtains
der Vorratsraum	derr for-rahts-rowm	store room
der Wald	derr valt	forest
die Walze	dee valtse(r)	roller
warten	varten	to wait
der Wärter	derr vehrter	keeper
waschen	vashen	to wash
die Waschmaschine	dee vash-masheene(r)	washing machine
ins Wasser springen	inss vasser shpringen	to dive
der Wasserfall	derr vasser-fall	waterfall
die Wasserkresse	dee vasser-kresse(r)	watercress
der Wasserskiläufer	derr vasser-shee-loyfer	water skier
der Wassertrog	derr vasser-troak	water trough
der Wecker	derr veker	alarm clock
der Wegweiser	derr vayg-vyzer	sign post
der Wein	derr vyne	wine
weiß	vyss	white
der Weltraum	derr velt-rowm	space
werfen	vairfen	to throw
um die Wette laufen	oom dee vette(r) lowfen	to race
wild	vilt	fiercely
die Winde	dee vinde(r)	winch
die Windmühle	dee vint-mewle(r)	windmill
wir	veer	we
der Wissenschaftler	derr vissen-shaftler	scientist
der Wohnwagen	derr voan-vahgen	caravan
der Wolf	derr volf	wolf
das Wrack	dass vrak	wreck
die Würstchen	dee vewrst-khen	sausages
wütend	vewtent	angrily
der Zaun	derr tsown	fence
das Zebra	dass tsaybra	zebra
die Zelte	dee tselte(r)	tents
die Ziege	dee tseege(r)	goat
die Ziegelsteine	dee tseegel-shtyne(r)	bricks
ziehen	tsee-en	to pull
die Zitronen	dee tsitroanen	lemons
der Zoll	derr tsoll	customs
der Zucker	derr tsooker	sugar
der Zug	derr tsook	train
die Zwiebeln	dee tsvee-beln	onions
zwischen	tsvishen	between

Pronunciation Guide

On these pages is the guide on how to say all the sentences in German in this book, using the same rules as on page 40.

Page 4 and 5 Inspektor Nomen und die geheimnisvollen Vorgänge auf dem Markt.
inspektor nomen oont dee gehymniss-follen forgenge(r) owf daym markt.
nomen gayt owf dayn markt, oom eynen deep tsoo finden.
err denkt: "vair ist dee keershen oont dee aird-bairen oont dee himbairen?"
err zeet zikh eyne(r) ananas an, lest eyne(r) meloane(r) fallen oont ist eynen apfel.
err gayt an dayn oronjen, dayn tsitroanen oont dayn aprikoazen forbye.
err showt dee beernen, dee trowben oont dee bananen an.
err blypt shtayen, oom owf eynen pfeerzikh tsoo drewken oont oom eyn pampelmooze(r) oont eyne pahr pflowmen tsoo kowfen.
"vair hat dee airpsen oont dee boanen oont dayn zalaht gegessen?"
nomen oonterzoocht dee kartoffeln oont dee muren oont dee koalku(r)pfe(r).
err tritt owf eyne(r) tomate(r), shtu(r)st eyne ku(r)p-khen foller piltse(r) oont eynen eymer mit vasserkresse(r) oom.
err showt hinter dayn rooben oont dayn roasenkoal hairfor oont kreekht an derr roaten bayte(r) forbye
err gayt an derr selleree forbye, oont zeet zikh dee radeez-khen oont dee tsveebeln an.
err rootsht owf eyner shtange(r) porray owss, shtolpert ewber eynen bloomen-koal oont findet dee deebe(r).

Page 6 and 7 Inspektor Nomen und die geshtoalenen Diamanten
inspektor nomen oont dee geshtoalenen dee-amanten
inspektor nomen fehrt tsoo daym shiff. err gayt dass fallreep hinowf oont shpricht mit daym kapitayn.
derr kapitayn ertsaylt eem, dass eynige(r) dee-amanten fon eynem deep geshtoalen vorden zint. ahber eyne(r) frow hat een gezayen.
nomen shlykht ewber dass deck oont fenkt dayn mann. ahber syne(r) tashen zint lehr.
derr deep hat dee dee-amanten owf daym shiff fershtekt. kannst doo zee finden?

Page 8 and 9 Wachtmeister Verb hat einen schweren Tag
vacht-myster fairp hat eynen shvairen tahk
fairp leekt im bett oont shlayft. err vacht owf oont shtykt owss daym bett.
err drayt dee vasser-krehne(r) owf, vesht zikh dee hende(r) oont rypt zyne gezikht troken.
err pootst zikh dee tsayne(r), tseet zynen shlahf-antsook owss, tseet zyne(r) klydoonk an oont bewrstet zikh dass hahr
fairp rootsht dass gelender hinoonter oont ist dann zyne frew-stewk.
err trinkt zynen kafay, leest dee tsytoonk oont lest eynen teller fallen.
err fewtert dayn kanahr-ee-en foagel, shleest dass fenster oont u(r)fnet dee tewr.
err fehrt mit zynem vahgen, gayt inss bewro oont shrypt eynen breef.
err shprikht am telefoan, err-tsaylt nomen fon eynen rowp-ewberfall oont loyft hinowss tsoo zynem vahgen.
err showt zikh eyne fenster an, zeet eynen fooss-shtapfen oont zoocht dayn eyne-brekher.
fairp verfolkt dayn eyne-brekher, fenkt een oont zee gerahten in eyne hant-gemenge(r).
derr eyne-brekher tritt fairp, fairp shlaykt dayn eyne-brekher, oont err fellt oom.
fairp haypt een owf, nimmt een tsoor politsye-vache(r) oont shpairt een eyne.

Page 10 Inspektor Nomen und der priesgekrönte Bulle
inspektor nomen oond derr pryz-gekru(r)nte(r) boole(r)
drye doome(r) deebe(r) ferzoochen, eynen pryz-gekru(r)nten boolen tsoo shtaylen. doorch velkhe(r) tore(r) gayt inspektor nomen, oom zee tsoo ertappen?

Page 12 und 13 Inspektor Nomen und die Fabrikspione
inspektor nomen oont dee fabreek-shpee-oane(r)
nomen shtayt drowssen for eyner fabreek vacher. err zeecht, vee tsvye spee-oane(r) herowss-lowfen.
err folkt eenen dee shtrahsse(r) hinoonter, doorch dass tor hindoorch oont in dayn park hineyne.

err loyft an daym zay, an dayn showkeln oont an derr marsh-kappele(r) forbye.
dee shpee-oane(r) zint bye eyne(r) shoole(r). nomen blickt doorch dass gitter oont zeet zee owf daym shool-hoaf.
err ferfolkt zee an derr keerkhe(r) forbye, oom dass keeno heroom oont in dass hoatel hineyne.
err findet dee shpee-oane(r) in eynem kafay. dann gayen zee tsoo derr ampel oont ewber-kvairen dee shtrahsee(r) an daym foossgenger-ewbergank.
zee varten an eyner booss-halte-shtelle(r). nomen loyft hinter eynen latairnen-pfahl oont fershtekt zikh hinter eyner shtahtoo-e(r).
dee shpee-oane(r) ferpassen dayn booss oont gayen tsoo fooss vyter an daym kranken-howss oont an eynem loch in derr shtrahsse(r) forbye.
zee zayen daym mann mit eynem press-looft-hammer tsoo, vairfen eynen blik owf eynen bagger oont eynen valtse(r).
zee shpringen ewber eynige(r) roaren oont tseegelshtyne(r). dah zayen zee nomen mit eynem politsisten.
zee rennen in eyn bewro, dass treppen-howss hinowf oont owf dee foyer-lyter.
nomen ferfolkt zee bis owf dass dach, oom eynen fahnenmast heroom oont ervisht zee shleesslikh bye eynem shorn-shtyne.

Page 14 and 15 Inspektor Nomen fliegt mit eine Düsenmaschine
inspektor nomen fleekt mit eyner dewzen-masheene(r)
inspektor nomen fehrt tsoom flook-hahfen. err ist owf derr zooche(r) nach eynem shmoogler.
err tsykt syne(r) flook-karte(r) for. err gayt doorch dayn tsoll oont lest synen pass ap-shtempeln.
err vartet in derr ap-flook halle(r), err bekommt zyne(r) board-karte(r). err zeet zikh dee anderen passajeerer an.
inspektor nomen gayt tsoor dewzen-masheene(r) hinowss. err gayt doorch dass flook-tsoyk bis tsoo eynem zits. err befestikt zynen zikher-hyts-goort.
dee dewsen-masheene(r) rollt ewber dee shtart-bahn oont errhaypt zikh in dee looft.
err shprikht mit daym peeloaten, veerft eynen blik owf dass instroomenten-brett oont gayt veeder tsoo-rewk dayn gank entlank.
err zeet dee golt-barren, darowfhin flewstert err derr stewardess etvas inss oar oont ferhaftet dayn shmoogler.

Page 16 Inspektor Nomen und der Kostümverleih
inspektor nomen oont derr kostewm-ferlye
nomen oont syne assistent gay-en tsoo eynem kostewm-ferlye. vee-feele(r) kostewme(r) probeeren zee an?

Page 18 and 19: Nomen und die Supermarktbande
nomen oont dee supermarktbande(r)
nomen gayt tsoom supermarkt. err ist owf derr zooche(r) nach laybens-mittel-deeben.
err gayt am broat oont an derr booter forbye oont zeet zikh dayn kayze(r) an.
err gayt an derr milkh oont am yogoort forbye oont lest eynige(r) eyer fallen.
err zeet dayn shinken oont dayn shpek an oont kreekht am fish forbye.
err blikt hinter dass mehl oont dayn tsooker oont dee shokolade(r).
err shtayt byme hoanik, showt zikh dee marmelade(r) an oont zoocht zikh eyne pahr zewssig-kyten owss.
err loyft an dayn koochen oont plets-khen forbye oont macht eynen groassen shritt ewber dee bru(r)-khen.
err shtu(r)st doazen oont flashen oont glayser oom. err root zikh bye derr gefreertroo-e(r) owss, tritt mit daym fooss gaygen eynem korp oond eynige(r) kartoanz.
nomen findet etvas flysh, eyne hewn-khen oont mairere(r) vewrst-khen.
err loyft an dayn kassen forbye, shprinkt ewber eyne pahr eyne-kowfs-tashen oont ewber eynige(r) zecke(r).
dann ervisht err dee deebe(r) err layt zee in eynen eyne-kowfs-vahgen oont brinkt zee inss hoonde(r)-gefengnis.

Page 20 Detektiv Präposition und das Gespensterschloß
daytekteef prepozit-see-oan oont dass geshpenster-shloss
daytekteef prepozit-see-oan gayt tsoo daym shloss. dort hahben gowner eynen shats fershtekt.
err kommt am vasser-grahben an, gayt ewber dee tsook-brewke(r) oont oonter daym tor-boagen hindoorch.
err showt oonter eynen shtyne, zoocht mit syner tashenlampe(r) nach daym shats oont loykhtet tsvishen tsvye kanoanen.
alss err bye eyner zoyle(r) shtayen blypt, hurt err shritte(r) inn derr naye(r) oont showt in eynem rowm.
eyne geshpenst errshynt hinter eem, oont dann shtayt es for eem. err loyft owf dee treppe(r) tsoo.
err shprinkt shnell hinoonter, fellt doorch dayn fooss-boaden, landet yedoch owf synen fewssen.

Page 21 Pronomen kommt zur Hilfe
pronomen kommt tsoor hilfe(r)